# Contents

C000120289

I wish to thank Lesley Clark in particular for her expert advice and guidance, and for reading and commenting on various drafts. Thanks are also due to Prue Goodwin and Viv Edwards for their help and encouragement.

**Judith Baxter**

Reading and Language Information Centre
University of Reading
Bulmershe Court
Reading RG6 1HY

ISBN 07049 14085

Designed and produced by Text Matters

# The question of gender

The issue of gender and schooling is rarely out of the news. In the past, politicians and educators struggled to make schools fairer places for girls. Equal opportunities policies ensured that *girls* were able to perform on an equal footing with boys in all areas of school life. Girls mature earlier than boys and often acquire literacy skills more quickly and effectively. Partly as a result of such factors, girls now outperform boys in most subject areas at all key stages. Today, issues of female equality have been eclipsed by concerns about *boys* and under-achievement, particularly in the area of literacy.

Teachers now face a real challenge about the teaching of gender. Schools feel they must boost the performance of boys not least because they have to meet demanding literacy targets. But this approach may unwittingly exclude the continuing needs of girls. Thus, teachers need to be aware of the whole picture – however complex this may seem. Gender differences should be viewed as one important aspect of pupil diversity. On one hand, in the spirit of inclusion, girls and boys are entitled to the *same* opportunities to achieve in the classroom. On the other hand, girls and boys do have very different learning needs that may require the use of *differentiated* learning strategies and experiences.

This book helps teachers to address the question of gender by drawing on best practice in line with the National Literacy Strategy. In particular, it looks at:

- the significance of gender (alongside other factors) in determining policies for the teaching of oracy and literacy
- what teachers need to know about the different ways in which girls' and boys' speak, listen, read and write
- what teachers can do to support the differentiated needs of girls and boys as language learners
- best practice in enabling teachers to raise literacy targets and to help underachieving boys.

# The significance of gender

'Girls can't play football'
'Don't be a sissy'
'Boys can't skip'
'Girls have tidier handwriting than boys'

Whether you believe that gender differences are natural, culturally produced, or a combination of the two, children quickly develop a gendered identity. From the moment they are born, children enter a world with very clear ideas about being male or female. The language and texts typically surrounding young children – such as birth cards, posters, adverts, comics, picture books, toy catalogues, TV images – categorise and represent them as boys or girls. Parents tend to make all sort of gender-based assumptions when they speak to their children. From an early age, girls and boys have a strong sense of what counts as feminine or masculine speech and behaviour and are keen to conform to these norms.

By the time children start school, both girls and boys have already begun to learn how to speak, read and write differently as a girl or a boy. Such learning continues throughout the school years and afterwards. Teachers often have different expectations of girls and boys. According to Myhill (2000), teachers are generally less positive about boys than girls, although they consider boys to be better risk-takers, to take the wider view of things, and to be more divergent in their thinking. Teachers also tend to speak differently to girls and to boys.

But this tendency to differentiate boys and girls may also have the danger of reinforcing gender stereotypes. If girls are always thought to be compliant, conforming and industrious, or boys to be unsettled, restless and physically active, this may limit the possibilities of what pupils can achieve. The point here is that teachers need to look for a sense of balance – girls and boys *are* different, but this should not limit our view of the possibilities of what they can learn.

## Girls – the disadvantaged sex?

According to research published this year, a woman who chooses not to have children and competes equally with men will still earn on average £100,000 less in a lifetime; a mother pays a female forfeit of £250,000. A non-manual male worker earns on average £525 a week, a woman only £345. Women are still penalised in work because the gatekeepers who judge ability are predominantly men. So in 1998, women comprised only 3.6% of directors. So it goes on and on.
*The Guardian*, 22 August 2000

In the 1970s and 1980s, the Equal Opportunities movement was concerned to eradicate *difference* between girls and boys. Its aim was an inclusive one – to provide the *same* educational opportunities for both sexes, and to tackle areas of school policy or practice that discriminated between girls and boys. It viewed difference as divisive because this symbolised the unequal relationship between girls and boys, the dominance of the male sex over the female.

One important focus of equal opportunities policies was upon the way language was used around the school – on signs, labels, posters, teaching resources, pupils' work, and in job titles. Language was seen to play an important part in either reinforcing or challenging gender stereotypes. There were concerns not only that boys and girls were represented in stereotyped roles, but so were male and female teachers. The Equal Opportunities Commission supported a number of self-help manuals which offered schools a framework for constructing policies of this kind. While purporting to represent the interests of both sexes equally, the emphasis in these manuals was upon the embedded sexism against *females*.

Myers (1992) suggests that the following areas of language use should be questioned in drawing up a policy.

### Spoken language

- How are staff addressed by colleagues – Mr, Dr, Ms, Miss or Mrs?
- How are pupils supposed to address staff
  - Miss, Sir, Madam, Marm?
- If the form of address indicates marital status for some members of staff but not for others, does this matter?
- Is use made of gender-specific terms – headmaster, senior mistress, dinner lady?

### Printed and written language

- How are pupils listed in registers? Is there a justification for listing girls and boys separately, or for listing boys first and girls second?
- Is the male pronoun 'he' generally used to refer to any of the people listed in handbooks about the work of the school?

### School environment

- Are labels on doors in the school gender-specific, e.g. headmistress? If so, what could be used instead?
- Are general notices for users of the building gender-neutral or gender-specific, e.g. 'Workmen should report to the office'?

Teaching resources were of particular concern. These were considered to favour the interests, needs and aptitudes of *boys* rather than girls. Reading programmes, such as the once universally popular *Ginn 360* and *One, Two Three and Away*, were consistently found to be discriminatory in their under-representation of female characters, as well as in their depiction of girls and women in traditional, stereotyped roles. Teaching materials of this type were considered 'sexist' because girls were often shown in private, domestic settings doing housework, caring for younger children or playing with dolls. Boys on the other hand, were portrayed as outgoing and adventurous, seeking challenges in the outside world. As a consequence of the backlash against such materials, educational publishers today rigorously monitor reading materials for numerical imbalances, use of gender stereotypes, sexist grammar, and so on. Yet it is worth asking whether the struggle for equal opportunities for girls has truly been won. If the current rhetoric on the boys and under-achievement issue is to be believed, it would certainly appear so.

## Underachieving boys?

 Boys are lagging behind in education
*The Guardian,* 17 August 2000

 Schools told to root out lad culture
*The Telegraph,* 18 August 2000

Since the 1990s, any concerns about sexist reading materials have been well and truly overtaken by the issue of boys and under-achievement. Government agencies (e.g. QCA, 1998; Frater, 2000) have produced booklets on the subject, and the National Literacy Trust maintains a database of initiatives in this area. There are also numerous individual projects in schools to target the needs of underachieving boys in particular. These initiatives tend to be characterised by:

- close involvement of parents and other adults
- use of male role models for reading
- promotion of self-esteem, order and responsibility
- good literacy practices at whole school level that take account of the needs of individual pupils
- local authorities providing strong support for their schools.

Recently, the current close focus on boys achievement has intensified in the light of schools' concerns to meet demanding literacy targets. However, unlike the drive for sameness and inclusion behind equal opportunities policies, the boys and underachievement campaign is concerned to *differentiate* boys from girls – to target and address boys' apparently different learning interests, needs and abilities.

Undoubtedly, there is a problem. By almost any standard of literacy, girls are now outperforming boys. Girls do better overall in pre-literacy skills, learn to read earlier, say they like reading more, read more widely than boys, spend more time reading independently, and perform better in all reading tests including SATs. Many theories have been advanced to explain the disparity in girls' and boys' achievement in literacy. One of the more favoured – ironic in the light of previous equal opportunities policies – is that classroom contexts are themselves feminised, in that they lack male role models in the shape of teachers, assistants and parent helpers. Within the feminised reading culture of the primary classroom, the reading materials on offer are unlikely to appeal to boys as they reflect the interests, themes and concerns of their predominantly female teachers.

There is no question that boys are among the poorest readers in our schools and that they need our help, but arguably, this has *always* been the case. It is well known that the numbers of boys referred to remedial services has always considerably exceeded the number of girls. But in the long term, it cannot be a good thing to weight policies of inclusion chiefly in favour of one sex or the other. It was often said that boys felt marginalised during the equal opportunities era of the 1970s and 1980s. But now girls may be experiencing a similar sense of alienation as their teachers direct their energies and resources towards boosting the boys. Millard (2000) has criticised this 'pro boy pro girl shoot out' where gender issues are seen as competitive, rather than as different aspects of the same social and educational questions. It now seems essential to 'balance the books' – to construct teaching policies that further the development of *both* sexes.

## Teaching for diversity

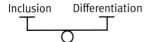

Inclusion    Differentiation

Within both the National Curriculum and the National Literacy Strategy there lies a tension between two forces. On one hand, the principle of *inclusion* stresses the similarities, connections and common goals between pupils, calling for all pupils, regardless of gender, class, ability and culture, to be able to participate fully within the curriculum. On the other hand, the principle of differentiation encourages teachers to distinguish between the individual *differences* of each of their pupils and to plan curricula accordingly.

Teachers can strike this delicate balance between girls' and boys' needs by drawing upon the many models of good practice of teaching for diversity, examples of which are given in the following chapters.

# Speaking of gender

DAVID: [to Elizabeth] Get them.
SIMON: We need four. Where are they? Get four, Nadia.
DAVID: We'll need some bits for the window, Elizabeth.
SIMON: Nadia, put one of those there.

Fisher, J. (1994) Unequal voices: gender and assessment. In D. Graddol et al (eds) *Researching language and literacy in social context.* Clevedon: Multilingual Matters for the Open University, pp.168–76

Girls and boys do not always have the same access to classroom talk, and they generally speak and listen in quite different ways. The introduction to the National Literacy Strategy (NLS) clearly states that effective teaching for the literacy hour is grounded in good oral work that 'enhances pupils' understanding of language in both oral and written forms and the way language can be used to communicate'. It is therefore important not only that girls and boys get equal access to opportunities to speak and listen – within the literacy hour as well as across the curriculum – but also that teachers ask children to reflect critically upon the role of gender, among other social factors, in determining how people communicate.

In developing pupils' critical literacy, teachers should be aware of the differences research has found in the way girls and boys communicate in the classroom. Some of the key patterns are:

- in whole class settings, boys tend to talk far more than girls, and exercise a range of strategies to gain and keep this attention. For example, boys are said to 'chip in' more to whole class discussion, and often use more confident expressions when they begin their turn ('I think I know...')
- when sitting on the floor, boys often take up the front and central positions where they are better placed to catch the teacher's eye.
- teachers usually give boys more attention than girls by asking them more questions, responding more to boys when their hands are up, and giving boys more 'air time' for their contributions.
- boys volunteer more, and get chosen to take on 'responsible' tasks to help the teacher, such as holding a class resource like a map for the rest of the class to see.
- in small, mixed sex groups, girls are often at a disadvantage. Fisher (1994) found boys always talked more than the girls. While the girls did get as involved as the boys in discussion, there was a group expectation that the *boys*' ideas were to be taken more seriously and adopted by the group.
- boys in mixed sex groups often tend to direct and instruct where there was a problem to be solved or work to be done. Girls often take up the role of fetcher and carrier.

- girls prefer a more co-operative and collaborative style of speaking when working in small groups, whereas boys tend to be more sparring and competitive.
- when working at the computer, boys tend to take over the control of the equipment, thus reducing the responsibility of girls for their work. If difficulties arise, boys are more likely to seek their own solutions whereas girls tend to depend on adult help.
- teachers often help girls but challenge boys to find their own solutions to a problem.

These are only general patterns. We can all think of quiet, reserved boys on one hand, and of articulate, assertive girls on the other. If you can help a 'difficult' boy to feel involved in a discussion with a question or a role that occupies or motivates him, he is less likely to disrupt the rest of the class. But this can have a knock-on effect, reinforcing boys as talkers and girls as listeners.

Teachers therefore need to be prepared to look quite closely at their own classroom practices in order to become more aware of the gender inequalities that form a part of routine classroom interactions. They should be aware that talk is a useful tool in engaging boys in a range of learning activities, but that the effect of encouraging boys may be to further marginalise the contributions of girls. Here are some ideas of good practice to enable both girls and boys to experience and reflect on different types of talk.

## A whole-school approach

The central role of talk across the curriculum and within the literacy hour needs to be prioritised as a whole school policy. This will require schools and individual teachers to build the following into their routine practices:

- Regularly planning at a whole school level the range of encounters pupils have with talk, and how these will be implemented within different subject areas across the curriculum.
- Observation, monitoring and evaluating of each pupil's experience of oral work to ensure that this values and takes account of their cultural identity and background (e.g. age, gender, ability, home language).
- Modelling different types of talk and their purposes within a range of learning contexts: as an independent oral activity, as a route to reading or writing, or as a follow-on from reading or writing.

## Monitoring whole class talk

The NLS has placed a much greater emphasis upon whole class activities, particularly during the literacy hour. Teachers are expected to involve and motivate all the pupils in their class by well focused questioning, encouraging and praising individual contributions, and promoting whole class discussion. NLS documents provide some suggestions about how teachers can effectively include children of different ages or abilities, pupils with special needs or pupils with English as an additional language. What they rarely mention is gender.

Arrange for another teacher, a teaching assistant or a learning support assistant to observe you in the classroom. They would be seeking to find out whether you give more attention to girls or to boys, and if so, whether you give different kinds of attention. Ask them to watch a routine activity such as circle time or a whole class discussion, with some specific questions on a simple tick list:

- Where have girls chosen to sit?
- Where have boys chosen to sit?
- Who do you select to speak?
- What do boys choose to talk about?
- What do girls choose to talk about?
- Who do you address by name?
- Who calls out/chips in and how do you tend to respond to them?
- Who do you reprimand and how?
- Who do you reward or praise and how?
- Who do you ask to help, and what kinds of jobs and responsibilities do you assign them?

## Talk in small groups

### Record of oral contributions
Again with the help of a colleague, parent or even an older pupil, it can be illuminating to keep a record of the number and types of contributions girls and boys make during a particular oral activity. For example, the following tick list could be used to observe and monitor a small group discussion to meet Key Stage 2 requirements:

| Sophie | Hassan | Catherine | Thomas | |
|--------|--------|-----------|--------|--|
| ☐ | ☐ | ☐ | ☐ | Takes turns |
| ☐ | ☐ | ☐ | ☐ | Makes relevant contributions |
| ☐ | ☐ | ☐ | ☐ | Explores |
| ☐ | ☐ | ☐ | ☐ | Reasons |
| ☐ | ☐ | ☐ | ☐ | Qualifies/justifies |
| ☐ | ☐ | ☐ | ☐ | Deals with opposing points of view |
| ☐ | ☐ | ☐ | ☐ | Summarises/reviews |
| ☐ | ☐ | ☐ | ☐ | Reaches agreement |

This can be solely for teacher information, or it can become a class evaluative activity. The observer can feedback their observations to help the group think about how to work more collaboratively, or to think about who is involved, who less so, and what the group feels they might do about it.

### Group composition and roles
When we group pupils to work together or use equipment together, what criteria for groupings do we use? Do we use the same criteria all the time? In mixed sex classrooms, it's important to have a policy of active teacher management on how pupils are grouped. Teachers might aim to place their pupils in different combinations, 'mixing and matching' such factors as gender, ability, linguistic background, interests, and so on. They must intervene to 'ring the changes' with group composition. Sometimes they may allow free choice, and sometimes intervene to organise different combinations of single sex and mixed sex groupings.

Often group activities require pupils to perform a range of different roles such as spokesperson, scribe, chairperson, helper, envoy, and so on. Teachers need to be aware that in mixed sex groups, girls often take up the more subordinate roles of assistant, fetcher and carrier or scribe. While some activities rightly allow pupils to choose the role they wish to do, in other activities it is important that teachers intervene so that both girls and boys experience a range of roles at different times. Again it is important to 'ring the changes', and this is not just a gender issue. Noisy or dominant girls might benefit from being appointed as a scribe, while a quiet or reticent boy might be asked to be a spokesperson.

## Talk round the computer

† What future is there for the information revolution in the UK if women fail to be as enthusiastic about the prospect as men?
Wilson, J., Davies, B., & Whittaker, R. (1999) *Young children, videos and computer games.* London: Falmer Press

Computers can often be a huge incentive to learning for boys. Talking round the computer can lead to oral presentations to the class, role-play and drama activities, further IT or text-based reading, or to writing assignments. However, girls can easily be 'peripheralised' in work around the computer. Therefore teachers need to intervene, as follows:

- organise seating arrangements in mixed group or pair work so that girls sit more centrally, or are selected to operate the 'mouse'
- challenge girls to work out solutions for themselves
- ask both girls and boys to reflect upon the group dynamics round the computer. For example, a teacher might ask, 'How well did you work together? Did anyone take charge? Who had the most ideas?'

## Tackling stereotypes and inequalities

† In Mrs Hind's class, pupils are writing their own sentences, each one including three words from the board. The word trios are:

| | | |
|---|---|---|
| boy | football | window |
| gorilla | cage | keeper |
| monkeys | coconuts | hunters |
| soldier | army | tank |

Several ask her about the words, so she reads through them. Says of 'soldier, army, tank': That's one for the boys really, I suppose.
Quoted in Swann, J. (1992) *Girls, boys and language.* Oxford: Blackwell

Teachers are very powerfully placed to intervene to tackle gender stereotyping as it routinely crops up in class. They should aim to:

- draw attention to common stereotypes: where assumptions are made about girls' or boys' speech, characteristics and behaviour which may be limiting, reductive or sexist
  - ('Boys are more noisy/boisterous/ technical/lazy...'
  - 'Girls are more quiet/reserved/ emotional/tentative...')
- intervene when pupils use sexist language. Obvious examples are assuming that the generic pronoun 'he' must stand for a person or an animal, or that 'man' or 'mankind' should stand for 'people'. Also, there are far more sexist terms of abuse to describe females than males which pupils may routinely use against each other, such as 'cow', 'dog', 'bitch' or 'tart'.

## Critical reflection about talk

The NLS advocates that teachers should be making the teaching of talk far more explicit during the literacy hour and during whole class get-togethers such as circle time. Teachers are themselves role models for different ways of talking. An increased awareness of gender alongside other factors that differentiate pupils, will help teachers to make explicit to pupils how the use of talk can at times disadvantage girls or at other times, boys. Teachers can teach about talk by:

- encouraging girls/less confident pupils to respond more confidently, for example, by nominating them to speak; giving them more time to respond; making sure they are seated more centrally in the class so that they are not on the sidelines
- enabling girls/less confident pupils to be more assertive in whole class settings. If they are to give an oral presentation, such pupils need to be given plenty of time to prepare, rehearse and practise speaking before the whole class, for example through the use of 'time out' sessions (e.g. NLS flier 2)

- modelling open-ended responses. Boys in particular need to learn that in whole class discussion, giving the 'right' answer is only one type of response. Developing a discussion requires pupils to be speculative, reflective, questioning and open-ended.
- Talking about talk: teachers can make the subject of gender differences in talk a subject of study in its own right. Here are some 'controversial' statements that you might encourage groups of pupils, particularly in the middle years, to discuss:

*Girl talk/boy talk*

- Girls talk more than boys.
- Boys interrupt conversations and discussions more than girls do.
- Teachers take more notice of boys.
- Boys talk more about their feelings than girls do.
- Girls are better listeners than boys are.
- Girls ask more questions than boys do.
- Girls are more likely to call out than boys are.
- Boys talk more loudly than girls do.
- Boys put their hands up quicker than girls do.

# Reading the difference

'You can't read a book when you are on a bike'.
Quoted in Holden, C. (2000) *Gender and achievement in the middle years.*
Paper presented at BERA conference, University of Exeter

It is often said that the reason why girls learn to read more quickly than boys, and to achieve better literacy test results is that girls and boys engage in different kinds of reading practices both at home and at school. Millard (1997) argues that there are three powerful spheres of influence upon emergent readers – the family, friendship groups in the community, and peer groups at school. From an early age, the reading time for girls is structured to include (usually) female members of the family, friends at home and at school, but for boys this is less the case. Schools themselves also promote versions of literacy that are more compatible with girls' interests and reading habits than boys'. Fiction is often 'privileged' in school reading – it preponderates in book corners and is the centre of reading programmes. A range of recent research in schools shows that:

- girls tend to get more practice at, and more experience of reading at home.
- mums rather than dads tend to read to their children or hear their children read aloud. This may reinforce the idea that literacy is regarded as a female domain
- parents may expect less of boys than girls in the area of literacy and may communicate these expectations to their children

- in nurseries, girls tend to get more practice at reading than boys. Hodgeon (1993) suggests this may be because girls are more likely to stay close to (female) adult staff and they therefore get to take more part in literacy-based activities
- more girls than boys say they enjoy reading, and regard it as a favourite pastime
- more boys than girls say they dislike reading as a pastime. Boys say they prefer sports, computer games and 'playing out'
- girls are more positive than boys about school activities associated with reading such as reading programmes, storybooks or class novels
- boys generally prefer non-fiction to fiction, such as comics, magazines, joke books, football books. They prefer to read factual books about how things work, or information books about hobbies, computers or sports. They make more limited fiction choices than than girls do, mainly opting for mystery, adventure, crime and science fiction
- girls may be missing out on reading the kinds of texts boys enjoy – information, media and electronic texts
- as girls and boys get older, the differences in reading preferences become more distinct.

While there are no 'quick-fix' solutions, here are some examples of good practice that aim to make the teaching of reading more 'boy-friendly' – without losing sight of the approaches that have enabled *girls* to succeed.

## A whole-school approach

Lesley Traves (2000), a headteacher, suggests that real change, by means of a whole school policy, requires a managed programme of reading. This takes time, hard work and commitment to a common aim. Such an approach is likely to have the following features:

- a literacy team that meets at regular intervals to discuss the needs of each class, to allocate teaching and support staff, and to plan, monitor and evaluate the initiatives in progress. This includes monitoring the *range* and balance of reading experiences children encounter (e.g. so that boys will read a broader range of genres than those they might prefer; so that both boys and girls experience a balance between ownership of their own reading and teacher guidance)
- offering differentiated types of support to readers by tight target-setting, monitoring and assessing of all pupils
- support teacher and classroom assistant time allocated to those who need one-to-one help, including disaffected or disinterested boy readers
- use of Reading Recovery trained teachers
- involvement of parents and families. Certain schemes (e.g. home-school reading partnerships; localised initiatives such as the 'Dads and Lads' reading project; Storysacks) have encouraged parents, and particularly fathers, to take an active interest in their children's reading development

- training for parents: 'hands-on' workshops to infant children's parents and carers to give them strategies for supporting children's reading
- promoting a reading culture around the school. Books can be displayed along the corridor, staircases and in cosy places where children can read quietly. Posters might equally display male and female authors as well as boy and girl readers. Success in reading should be celebrated as much for boys as girls in whole school contexts such as assembly
- seeing men as readers. Make opportunities to have male role models (authors, sportsmen, local figures, dads, male teachers) read aloud in front of the whole school or lead reading sessions with a class or a group
- pairing readers: schemes like Buddies, where older pupils read alongside younger pupils, or enthusiastic readers are paired with more reluctant readers, are likely to motivate boys.

## Managing the resources

Teachers need primarily to build on what boys and girls *want* to read, while aiming to widen the repertoire of books they are both prepared to read. Teaching resources and reading materials need to reflect the changing nature of contemporary texts, for instance by providing access to CD-roms and computer network services. There is now an excellent range of stimulating and challenging fiction that is recommended for boys, particularly reluctant and less able readers (*see Resource materials on page 24*). Other reading materials might include

- a good range of colourful, glossy, non-fiction books which include topics such as hobbies, jokes, space, computers and sports, as well as 'fun' information books (e.g. *100 Nasty Facts about the Victorians*)

- newspapers, magazines and comics
- curiosity kits: innovative, non-fiction reading kits including book, artefact, magazine, stickers, and activities (*see Resource materials on page 24*)
- fiction that children themselves would choose to read for leisure. This may include popular genre series of school, adventure, mystery, horror or ghost books such as Goosebumps, media-inspired texts, graphic novels, or popular authors such as Jackie Wilson, Babette Cole or Quentin Blake

- media and electronic texts including educational TV programmes, films, computer games and guided access to the internet.

## Providing a social environment for reading

Many teachers have suggested that a vital way to motivate more reluctant readers, especially boys, is to make reading a more active and social business in the classroom. Francoise Fokias (2000), a middle years teacher, has argued for the need to create 'a warm, social context around reading which [is] an undisturbed time'. She found that in her use of *literature circles*, the physical context of reading as a group in a carpeted area well supplied with books, encouraged a sense of physical closeness, intimacy and social contact among her pupils. More importantly, she suggests that boy readers in the middle years may find lone, independent reading

difficult – they need to interact socially more, to experience a sense of social cohesion when they read.

Paired or group reading, whether incorporated in the literacy hour, or as part of reading circles, enables reluctant boy readers to 'buy into' the business of reading. It enables boys to gain access to certain types of book that they might not otherwise read. Here the role of interactive talk is critical. They learn to hear the more sophisticated story-telling techniques of their teacher, to listen to their peers read, to read aloud themselves, to voice their views on a book, and gradually to discuss with their teacher the more technical aspects of fiction such as characterisation, plot, themes and vocabulary. Boys and girls also enjoy making tapes of themselves and others reading.

## Structuring reading activities

It is now something of a cliché that boys are said to respond to a more structured approach to reading activities than girls appear to do, but the approach of Greg Wallace (2000), a Year 6 teacher is given here as an example of good practice.

Such an approach is likely to include the following features:
- *Generating interest in books and authors.* Wallace achieved this by enthusiastically introducing a book on which the class was going to work. Once the reading of the book was under way, he used the author as a focus to link and introduce

other books by the author or of a similar theme, reading the first chapter or two and leaving the books for children to read.

- *Ownership of reading:* boys in particular need to be encouraged to be more proactive in selecting texts that interest them, rather than always depending on teacher guidance. Their voluntary choices need to be valued and supported rather than criticised.

- *Modelling reading strategies.* Wallace aimed to make explicit to the class the processes that readers go through, such as locating different kinds of books, making decisions about how to select books that are interesting and readable, dealing with 'difficult' words and passages, finding information in non-fiction texts, skimming, scanning, reading in close detail, and note-taking.

- *Protected reading time:* while there is a place for guided or shared reading activities, this should be balanced by the use of guarded time for individual pupils to read in  an uninterrupted, silent, sustained way. While this is often easier for girls,

it provides a structured opportunity for boys to make a commitment to the reading of longer texts.

- *Creating opportunities for communication about individual reading:* Wallace is one of many teachers who has experimented with the use of a reading journal for a more structured set of responses to texts. His approach was to design the journal to work as a double spread: one page for children to record their comments on their reading, and the other page to undertake activities:

*Reading journal activities*

- A box for interesting words
- A space to draw a picture of a character or scene from a book – and explain it
- A box to record examples of good writing
- A space to design a poster to advertise a book
- A box to write five examples of fact or opinion from a piece of writing
- A grid to design a word search
- A space to say how a character feels in a situation
- A box in which to write a quiz about the book

## Critical reflection about reading

Teachers can aim to make gender an explicit topic of interest in its own right. When children start to look at different genres of fiction (such as fable, fairy tale or animal stories), and explore common narrative structures (such as quests, romance, riddle tests and rescues), they can be encouraged to discuss the way such stories reveal different and unequal forms of identity for male and female characters.

*Gender identities in fairy/
folk stories*

- Draw two columns
- List all the activities that the main female character does
- List all the activities that the main male character does
- What do they do that is similar?
- What do they do that is different?
- Now retell/rewrite the story, but swap the male and female characters' (e.g. Rapunzel/the Prince) parts in the stories. ('One day, a beautiful prince looked down from the tower...')
- Tell or read your new version aloud
- What effect does this have?
- Why does it work/not work?

Children can read books with alternative images and messages – such as non-sexist fairy tales – and by comparing these books with more traditional versions can use this as springboard for discussion of gender issues (*see Resource materials on page 24*).

• Children can be asked to question the choices of books they prefer reading. A middle years class might do a survey of the class's reading interests, such as favourite authors, genres, subjects, characters, story lines. Pupils can be asked to make comparisons between the preferences of girls and boys, and to discuss the reasons why they think there are differences. Should girls be asked to read more non-fiction and information books? Should boys be asked to read school or animal fiction?

# Writing the difference

What boys like is unambiguously heroic heroes, impeded in performance only by physical injury. Complexities of moral relationships or unglamorous struggles with imperfection do not interest them: their taste is for swift, decisive and violent action triumphing over unequivocally evil opposition.

Thomas, P. (1994) Gender and genre: reading routes to writing. *The English and Media Magazine,* 31: pp. 18–24

It is in the area of school writing that gender differences seem most apparent, because this is where the underachievement of boys manifests problems across the whole curriculum. The previous two chapters have stressed how vital it is for teachers to draw upon the interrelatedness of talk and reading to support and develop children's writing. This book has so far stressed that the answer to concerns about male underachievement lies in the principles of best practice. This means implementing a whole school policy of reflective action – continuously observing, planning, monitoring and evaluating pupils' access to writing experiences.

From the nursery class and infant school onwards, girls and boys appear to be distinctively different as writers. First, they make different writing *choices* – choices about what, when and how they write. Both girls and boys make such choices and draw their ideas for writing upon the reading and viewing culture to which they subscribe. These will include gender-differentiated comics, popular fiction, TV programmes and computer games. Research findings about girls' and boys' writing choices provides the following picture.

- Girls appear to like writing activities more than boys, and in their early years, often select writing in a 'free choice' area. As part of the National Writing Project (1990), Herring found that in nursery schools, boys tended to avoid the 'writing area' whereas girls tended to make frequent appearances.
- As boys grow older, they often express a dislike of writing, especially the kinds of imaginative writing they have to do for English.
- While girls tend to favour story and imaginative writing, boys tend to prefer more factual and informative writing arising out of a particular project. This is a tendency that becomes more marked as children progress through school.
- In imaginative writing, girls are more likely to focus on the emotions, motivations and relationships of characters using a combination of narrative, description and dialogue. Contexts are often strongly developed including aspects of familiar, local or communal living – in a school, home, stable or hospital.
- Boys are more likely to focus on a strong plot-line focused on power struggles between sketchily drawn characters, and on bloodthirstiness or violence. Their stories are often set in futuristic,

surreal or fantasy locations or in settings derived from TV programmes or computer games.

- Girls are prepared to experiment with using a much wider range of genres and writing styles than boys.

Secondly, girls and boys *perform* differently as writers. SATs results since 1995 consistently show that girls generally perform better than boys across the range of writing and spelling tasks at both Key Stage 1 and 2. Boys often produce better written responses to questions that are closed and factually-based (e.g. 'Make a list of...'), and are therefore better at tasks that ask them to inform and explain. Girls, on the other hand, produce better written responses to questions that are open-ended and expressive ('Say how you feel about...') and are thus better at tasks that ask them to imagine and explore feelings and ideas.

Recently, there has been concern (e.g. OFSTED, 1993; QCA, 1998) about boys' comparative lack of competence as writers – often perceived to be a maturation issue. On a compositional level, the creative quality and conceptual complexity of their work is said to be weak. Their ability to structure complex and extensive texts is much less developed than girls. They tend to dislike the drafting process, and prefer to produce a one-off piece. Girls often write far more extensively than boys, although this is not necessarily a measure of quality. On

a transcriptional level, boys' control of standard written English grammar is often insecure and their handwriting – particularly under test conditions – can often be indecipherable. They are reported to experience systematic failures to spell and punctuate.

Partly in response to target setting for literacy by the QCA and the National Literacy Strategy (NLS), teachers and educators have been working on various models of good practice that will boost boys' performances in writing whilst supporting the achievements of girls. Here are some of their suggestions.

## Becoming literate through play

During the early years boys come to literacy from a rather different position to girls. Literacy activities rest on a variety of other symbolising activities such as imaginative and fantasy play, drama work, drawing, modelling and construction activities. Whereas boys tend to use modelling and play as the way to develop their narratives, girls tend to develop their stories then express their ideas through play. Arguably, the different ways in which boys learn to become literate have not only been much misunderstood, but also undervalued. Two practitioners have suggested how teachers can build on the ways in which boys become literate, as follows:

- **Kate Pahl** (2000) found that boys in particular respond to map-making and construction as a way of expressing their ideas. Map-making (e.g. treasure maps) can often be woven in with narrative play – it is a way of telling the story through drawing or diagrams. Or it can be seen as a description of active play – drawing can represent particular actions. Her view is that map-making, modelling and construction activities are all acts of 'writing': they can be 'read' as the stories boys create, of equal value to girls' written narratives.

- **Penny Holland** (1999) discovered that teachers can build on boys' interest in war/weapons/superhero/transformation games as a bridge to play-script or story writing. She recognises that women teachers in particular feel alienated by play activities that are seen as noisy, physical and aggressive. But she argues that it would serve boys better if teachers were to get down on their hands and knees and join in. By introducing 'crawling, creeping, tiptoeing, whispering, gesture, co-operation and delegation', teachers can both be involved in boys' play, help to develop it and initiate some elementary critical inquiry:

    We can usefully intervene, after careful observation, in order to empower the boys to 'write' their own play scripts in the service of their imaginative and symbolic development, rather than in the limiting service of the macho media machine.

## Structuring writing activities

In parallel with the teaching of reading skills, boys in particular often benefit from a greater structuring of how writing is taught, which happens to coincide with recommendations for the teaching of the NLS. Here are some principles of good practice.

### Audience, purpose and context

Boys often benefit from being provided with purposeful frameworks for each writing activity. They should be asked to make organised choices when they are about to start a piece of writing, responding to questions such as:

- Who is the audience/readership for this piece?
- Why are you writing this story/letter/report?
- Which context is the writing for? Is it
    - to be put up on a wall display
    - to be part of a project
    - to be part of an assessment
    - to be read out in assembly?

### Text is context

The teaching of reading and writing is characterised by the need for meaningful contexts. Boys in particular need to see a clear point in any act of learning, and one way this can be effectively achieved is by teaching particular writing skills (e.g. writing a letter, spelling patterns) as they arise naturally from the texts studied as part of text level work. However word and sentence level work should not *always* arise from text work, as this can destroy the magic of the reading and writing experience.

### Fun and games

The teaching of word and sentence level work, when taught on its own, should be active, participatory, shared, enjoyable and contain an element of competition ('Who can be the fastest to find 10 words to describe...?'). Lessons need pace, purpose and structure if more reluctant boys are to respond. Here are some ideas:

- Display posters (which can be marked up)
- Rhyming songs, jingles, raps
- Use percussion instruments to reinforce phonic rules
- Competitive team games
- Marking each other's work
- Time limits
- Flat-texting (using highlighter pens to mark up features in a text)
- Collections of word cards to find spelling patterns
- Show me cards
- Washing lines (to peg up word or letter cards)
- Whiteboards used in pairs (to think, write, show)

### The writing process

Girls are far more motivated than boys about engaging with the process of drafting, revising, redrafting, editing and presenting a piece of writing.

Boys, in contrast, prefer to dash off a one-off piece. Julie Carr (2000) has argued that boys need to understand what it is like to be a 'real' writer by drawing on writers' workshop methods. This means having extended, uninterrupted time in which to write. But it also means breaking the writing process down into a number of stages, which are not overwhelming. Each stage ('how to draft', 'how to revise') might be given a separate 'slot' over a period of time. Here the use

of other adults can help to remove the stress of transcription. More reluctant writers might draft their work orally (to an adult or on to a tape); draft in pairs, or use a word-processor.

### Guided writing

Boys often respond to the challenge of writing if it is structured as a shared or collaborative experience, yet is closely orchestrated by the teacher. Jonathon Rooke (2000) in his work with middle years pupils found that the use of guided writing enabled him to work with small groups of children on specific writing techniques tiered to their needs, such as developing a character sketch, or crafting a sentence. The principles of guided writing – a clear focus, close supervision, a sequence of specific tasks, a collaborative enterprise, and a chance for immediate feedback on written work – have been found to motivate boys who are reluctant to write.

## Exploring voice

First person narrative writing has been a very popular vehicle for encouraging both boys and girls to write from their own experience. It is often assumed to develop children as individuals by helping them to project an individual 'voice', but teachers need to be aware that this can actually reinforce gender stereotypes if used as a routine tool. Pupils may be encouraged to take on a *range* of voices in their writing – female or male, adult or child, young or old, animal or human. If a class is asked to tell a story from the point of view of an animal, it may be asked to consider whether it might be better told from a female or a male perspective, and to reflect on the class responses if they are stereotyped.

As a route to writing, Patrice Baldwin (2000) advocates working in role with middle years pupils in order to challenge received ideas and stereotypes. Teachers can adapt Baldwin's ideas for exploring different voices, characters, motivations, by asking children to explore gender roles. Girls can be given male parts, and boys female parts. A scene from a story can be re-enacted using an all-boy or all-girl cast. Teachers can help children to explore their feelings afterwards. Why did they feel the scene was:

- funny
- embarrassing
- awkward
- unworkable
- workable?

## Critical reflection about writing

Both girls and boys can be asked to review their own work and those of their peers in terms of its reliance on gender (and other) stereotypes in the same way that people might review other published sources:

 *Reviewing pupils' or published work*

- Who did you think this piece of work was written for?
  - How can you tell?
- Is the subject matter more likely to appeal to girls or to boys?
  - How can you tell?
- If this is a story, how many male and female characters are there?
- What are the female characters doing?
- What are the male characters doing?
- How might the story be made to appeal more to:
  - boys
  - girls?

# End note

The National Literacy Strategy has provided a golden opportunity to spotlight the needs of underachieving boys as teachers strive to develop best practice in the classroom. But in the pursuit of exciting new approaches to motivate reluctant boys, it's important not to overlook a minority of (often quite able) under-achieving girls. They remain an invisible and often ignored group in the classroom because they are silent, self-effacing and undemanding. As they grow older, these under-performing girls often slip into the lower ability sets at secondary school.

How can we target boys without overlooking the girls? The answer lies in a whole school policy of reflective practice that is guided by a commitment to balance, fairness and pupil diversity. Only by a planned cycle of observation, monitoring, and evaluation – of the differentiated needs of all pupils, plus of the range of curricular provision, can teachers be sure that no child is marginalised. This is a time-consuming business. But if reflective practice of this type becomes a matter of routine, all children are likely to benefit, regardless of age, ability, gender or cultural background.

## References

Baldwin, P. (2000) Working in role. *The Primary English Magazine* 5, 5: 20–3

Barrs, M. & Pidgeon, S. (1998) *Boys and reading*. London: Language Matters, CLPE

Barrs, M. (1998) Texts and subtexts: literacy, gender and achievement. In M. Barrs & S. Pidgeon (1998), pp. 1–8

Carr, J. (2000) Extended writing: process is power. *The Primary English Magazine* 6, 1: 7–11

Fisher, J. (1994) Unequal voices: gender and assessment. In D. Graddol, J. Maybin & B. Steirer (eds) *Researching language and literacy in social context*. Clevedon: Multilingual Matters for the Open University, pp.168–76

Fokias, F. (2000) Changing practice through reflection. In M. Barrs & S. Pidgeon (eds) London: CLPE, pp. 23–8

Frater, G. (2000) *Securing boys' literacy*. London: The Basic Skills Agency

Hall, C. & Coles, M. (1999) *Children's reading choices*. London: Routledge

Hodgeon, J. (1993) Talking to parents. In M. Barrs & S. Pidgeon (eds) *Reading the difference* London: CLPE, pp. 49–56

Holland, P. (1999) Just pretending: developing boys' dramatic play in the nursery. *Language Matters* Spring: 2–5

Millard, E. (1997) *Differently literate: boys, girls and the schooling of literacy*. London: The Falmer Press

Millard, E. (2000) Confronting the gender question: a review article. In *The English and Media Magazine*, 41: 43–5

Myers, K. (1992) *Genderwatch! After the Reform Act*. Cambridge: Cambridge University Press

Myhill, D. (2000) Boy zones and girl power. *Curriculum* 10, 2: 86–99

National Writing Project (1990) *What are writers made of? Issues of gender and writing*. Walton-on-Thames: Nelson

OFSTED (1993) *Boys and English*. London: OFSTED

QCA (1998) *Can do better: raising boys' achievement in English*. London: QCA

Pahl, K. (1999) *Transformations: making meaning in nursery education*. Stoke on Trent: Trentham Books

Rooke, J. (2000) Guided writing: the point of production. *The Primary English Magazine* 6, 1: 25–29

Traves, L. (2000) Boys catch up and overtake. *Literacy Today* 24: 14

Wallace, G. (2000) Creating skilled readers. In M. Barrs & S. Pidgeon (eds). London: CLPE, pp. 13–18

## Resource materials

*Publishers produce lists of recommended texts for boys for example:*

Cooling, W. (1999) *Boys do read! A Puffin booklist*. London: Puffin Books

Random House Children's Books (1999) *Great books for boys*. London: Random House (www.randomhouse.co.uk)

*Book suppliers offer boxed selections and useful catalogues, for example:*

Books for Students Ltd (www.bfs.co.uk)

Badger Publishing (www. badger-publishing.co.uk)

*Local library authorities provide lists of resources, for example:*

Leicestershire County Council (2000). *Books with boy appeal: encouraging readers* 9–14. Tel: 0116 267 8000; also reading projects (Hampshire County School Library Service, *Dads and Lads*)

Young Book Trust offers independent advice on children's reading materials. Tel: 020 8516 2984

The Federation of Children's Books provides booklists – www.fcbg.mcmail.com

National Support Project for Story Sacks offers workshops for parents reading with their children. Tel: 01793 421168

The University of Plymouth, Rolle School of Education are piloting Curiosity Kits – a new reading model for boys and reluctant readers